Hans Kaldenbach

Act Normal!

99 Tips
for Dealing with the Dutch

with illustrations by Dragan Strišković

Translated from the Dutch by J.G. Knecht

2000 Prometheus Amsterdam

special thanks to::

Chams Berragiy, Karina Boom, Ian Holman, Yaron Kaldenbach, Aydın Kıllı, Adalet Yilmaz Kumçu, Thom Langerak, Helga Ravier, Orsine Resida, Gitta Verhoeven en Selahattin Zorlu.

First printing 1995
Seventh printing 2000

Original title *Doe maar gewoon*

Omslagontwerp Gerard Hadders
Illustraties Dragan Strišković
ISBN 90 5333 375 4

Introduction

Do you have contact with the Dutch in daily life?
If so, it is important to be familiar with some of their customs. The fact that some of them seem strange and inappropriate to you is probably due to differences between Dutch culture and your own. To the Dutch, your culture may also seem strange and inappropriate.
Here are tips for dealing with Dutch[1] men and women. They can serve as a concise and useful manual for the many foreigners who have settled in the Netherlands. And it is indispensable for the many tourists who come to visit our country every year.

Are you Dutch?
In that case, take a good look in the mirror. Enjoy the sight. Feel the astonishment and surprise: this is how others view you.

Readers from the provinces of Limburg and Brabant say the title should be: Dealing with Hollanders (those living in the provinces of North and South Holland).
When you have lived in the Netherlands a bit longer, you will understand why.

---

1 By 'Dutch' we mean 'white' Dutch men and women. You probably – incorrectly, I might add – assumed this.
For easy reading, the male form of address will be used.

1
Introducing yourself

Perhaps you are accustomed to introducing yourself with your first name. In the Netherlands this may seem odd. If you introduce yourself with your first name, some Dutch will think Achmed is your last name. If you're somewhere to do business, you always use your last name. In an informal setting, mention your first and last names.
In the Netherlands, soccer players and politicians are also always referred to by their last names.

2
Formal and informal forms of address

Many Dutch adults find it impertinent if you address them with 'jij', the informal 'you'. Only friends and acquaintances are allowed to say 'jij' to each other. In the beginning, the best policy is to use 'u', the formal form of address, with all adults (anyone older than 20 or so). After you've known each other for a while, your Dutch acquaintances will suggest switching to the informal 'jij'. Most Dutch will be offended if you use the informal 'jij' too soon.

3
They keep their distance

While talking to you, the Dutch maintain a greater distance than you are accustomed to. If *you* keep the distance Turks, Moroccans or Surinamese are used to, the Dutch will find this intrusive.
If a Dutch conversation partner takes a step back, it means he is uncomfortable. He feels that you are standing too close. If you are standing too close to a Dutch woman, she might interpret this as sexual interest.
Dutch people do not touch each other while having a conversation. If *you* touch *them*, you will notice that they find it unpleasant: they will think you are homosexual or don't know how to behave properly.

④ Punctuality

Dutch people often keep track of the exact time. And, in general, they are punctual. If *you* are late, this irritates them very much. The Dutch equate not being on time with not being trustworthy; they can't count on you. A Dutchman does not want to do business with such a person. A person who is late for a job interview will not be hired.
The Dutch do not know a lot about 'foreigners'. But they do know that foreigners are frequently late. That annoys them. 'Here I am, on time, and Hassan still isn't here,' they might say. If you want to get anywhere in the Netherlands, you have to learn to be punctual!

Tips:
– Always be on time. In the Netherlands, it is better to be ten minutes early than five minutes late.

– If you make an appointment with a Dutch person, write it down in your appointment book. This will make the Dutchman feel confident that you will honor the appointment.
– If you cannot come, give as much advance notice as possible. The Dutch like to know about a cancelled appointment several days in advance if possible.

5
Do not interrupt

In the Netherlands, it is considered good manners to let the other person finish what he is saying. In some countries, being attentive means talking simultaneously. But the Dutch consider it polite to wait until the other person is finished. Then the other speaker gets a turn. This is particularly true of Dutch people from the higher classes. If a Dutchman is interrupted, he might say: 'Let me finish talking, please', or 'You interrupted me'. In reaction, the other party will usually excuse himself and allow the speaker to finish.

6
'Yes' means 'yes': it's a commitment

If a Dutchman answers 'yes' to something, he's made a commitment. You, on the other hand, might say 'yes' to be polite or to indicate that you heard what was said. Or your 'yes' might have been a way to avoid a fight, an argument, or friction.
To the Dutchman, 'yes' is a commitment to something. The Dutch find it extremely irritating that many foreigners say 'yes' without feeling that they have agreed to anything. A Dutchman usually keeps his word, even when it is not to his advantage to do so.

'Ali, can you come tomorrow at nine o'clock?'
'Sure.'
'All right, agreed.'
The Dutchman believes concrete plans have been made!

(7)

Verbal versus nonverbal communication

The Dutch mainly pay attention to your literal words. They don't hear the intonation with which you say something. If you casually mention that something will happen tomorrow, they think it really will happen. If you mumble a halfhearted 'yes' in response to something a Dutchman suggests, he thinks you agreed to it. He won't have noticed your nonverbal 'I'd rather not'. The Dutch don't understand your reluctance to spoil the atmosphere with a blunt 'no'; they've learned to disregard nonverbal signals. They go by *what* you say, not *how* you say it.

8

Dropping by unannounced

The Dutch almost never visit each other without making an 'appointment' first. This includes close friends. Even a mother will phone her daughter to find out when it's convenient to come by. People almost never drop by unannounced. The same rules apply to family: first you ring them up ('How would it be if we came by today?'). If your visit would be inconvenient, your host will simply tell you so: 'No, today isn't a good day. Come another time if you like.' The Dutch do not consider this rude or blunt, but 'honest'. In these situations, honesty is considered more important than tact.
The Dutch also like to know exactly when you intend to arrive. That gives them time to tidy up the room, send the children to bed and have a steaming cup of coffee ready when you ring the doorbell.

9

Bringing a bouquet

In Holland, visitors frequently bring a bouquet of flowers. These are for the hostess, who will usually remark: 'You shouldn't have!' Although it sounds ungrateful, it is a way of expressing appreciation. During the visit, your bouquet will be placed in a vase, usually by the lady of the house.
It is particularly important to bring flowers if you don't know the people very well: this is almost guaranteed to make a good impression. In recent years the custom of bringing a bottle of wine as a gift has also become popular.

10

You won't automatically be asked to stay for dinner

If you visit a Dutch family at around five-thirty p.m., chances are you will not be asked to join them for dinner. Your Dutch hosts will find it quite normal to begin eating (at six o'clock) without you and will become rather uneasy because they don't understand why you don't leave.
Is that inhospitable? Not to the Dutch. Only very good friends or family members stay for dinner.
As a Dutchman, you would never pay someone a visit after four o'clock p.m. Most Dutch households will not be prepared to see visitors until after eight p.m.

A considerate Dutch host:
'It's six o'clock. We're going to eat now.
Would you like a cup of coffee?'

11

Not everything revolves around food

You will discover that Dutch cuisine is not terribly varied and that food does not occupy a prominent place in the Netherlands. The attitude is more one of 'eat to live' than 'live to eat'. The Dutch do not tend to spend an inordinate amount of time preparing a meal. When the Dutch say: '*What* we eat doesn't really matter as long as there's lots of it', there is some truth to it.

12

Enjoyment seems like a sin

Many Dutch find it difficult to enjoy the good things in life; it is as though they consider enjoyment a sin. They seem to have an internal 'barrier' that prevents them from enjoying things fully or letting themselves go. This is evident in their uninspired eating habits, inconspicuous clothing, sober architecture, restrained manner of celebrating, and so on. In Dutch history, the influence of Calvinism (a religious doctrine) has played a considerable role. The Dutch themselves say that Calvinism is to blame for their inhibitions regarding enjoyment, having fun, and expressing emotion.

13

Act normal!

In Holland, exhibiting material wealth is frowned upon. It is often difficult to judge who's rich and who's poor by the clothes people wear. Displaying expensive cars and jewelry is considered vulgar. To many Dutch men and women, it is a virtue to blend in with the crowd. People who want to be the best, reach the top, or excel in some way do not talk about it in public. These ambitions are almost something to feel ashamed of.

A very frequently used expression is: 'Act normal, that's odd enough!'

14

Who pays in a café or restaurant?

When the Dutch go out to eat together, it is quite usual to 'go Dutch': everyone pays for their own food and drinks. The Dutch do not consider this peculiar. To them, it is 'fair'. When you pay for your own food and drinks, you're free to order something expensive because nobody else has to help foot the bill. Of course frugality, a reluctance to pay for another's expensive tastes, also plays a role.

In a café, people are expected to take turns in buying drinks. Most Dutch will carefully keep track of who has already bought a round and who has not.

15

Annoyance if you speak your native tongue

A Dutchman will find it extremely annoying and inappropriate if you converse with others in your native tongue in his presence. It can arouse feelings of suspicion: he may think you're talking about *him*. Yet you would probably like to go on speaking your own language in such a situation, because you feel more at home with it. What should you do?

– If you're talking to several compatriots, one of you can speak Dutch to the Dutchman. Or:

– You or a conversation partner can say: 'Excuse us. We'd like to talk in our own language for a moment.' In most cases, the Dutchman will not feel he's being excluded.

16

Family ties are less important in the Netherlands

To many Dutch, family ties are becoming less important. Grandparents, aunts and uncles no longer play an important role in their lives. One's own family has priority, not the extended family. There is also a growing tendency to regard friends and acquaintances as more important than family. A Dutchman might say: 'Just because you have a brother or sister doesn't mean you have a good relationship with them.'

The Dutch probably do not inquire about *your* family very often either. Nor do they do this among themselves, men least of all. Friends often do not know the vital statistics of each other's families: whether parents are still living, how brothers and sisters are doing, and so on. The Dutch see nothing unusual in having their parents move to an old folks' home. Most elderly parents do not *want* to live with their children; they think their children are entitled to lead their own lives.

Families with a handicapped child sometimes place the child in a special home. The Dutch consider this a good solution to the problem: the child is in good hands. Their choice is in no way motivated by lack of compassion or humanity.

17

The weather

The Dutch spend a lot of time talking about the weather. Many conversations begin with: 'Nice weather, isn't it?' Or: 'By God, it just won't clear up, will it?' If you want to strike up a conversation with a stranger, talk about the weather: you can't go wrong.

Many people complain about the weather, but most Dutch wouldn't like to live in another climate.

18

Adorable little rogues

The Dutch find it amusing when children make cheeky remarks. They think that's healthy precocity. A child bold enough to make such remarks will be able to make its way in the big wide world. It can defend itself. Cheeky children are also quite popular in TV commercials. This does not mean that children can say anything they want. There are restrictions, but children do not have an easy time discovering what their limits are.

Cheeky Dutch children will probably be more irritating to you than to the Dutch.

19

To bed on time and no playing outside after six p.m.

To the Dutch, 'bedtime' is an important aspect of raising children. A seven-year-old, for example, knows that he has to go to bed at a quarter past seven. And Dutch children go to bed on time, not five minutes late!

Dutch parents also consider it very important that children do not play outside after six p.m. Only on warm summer evenings may children play outside until nine. The Dutch often refer to parents who allow their children to play outside until late as 'antisocial': 'Those people do not know how to raise their children properly.'

These child-raising values are very firmly instilled in Dutch culture. As a result, they frequently clash with Turkish and Moroccan ideas as to what the proper bedtime is.

What does a Dutchman consider a 'nice' neighborhood?
One where all the children are indoors after six p.m. and where people put the garbage out after dark.

(20)

Everything according to plan

The Dutch lead very planned lives.
At ten-thirty a.m. they drink coffee.
Lunch (usually sandwiches) is around one p.m.
At approximately three p.m. they drink coffee or tea.
At six p.m. most people eat their hot evening meal.
At eight p.m. they watch the news.
At approximately eleven p.m. most Dutch people go to bed.
Rituals concerning life's emotional events are also carefully planned and orchestrated.
Funerals follow a standard scenario, with the length of each part precisely planned in advance. The same is also true of weddings and other festivities.

21
Sex

In the Netherlands, sex is discussed more openly than in many other countries. The Dutch are also less inhibited about nudity, for example on the beach or in the sauna. After sports, they sometimes shower together naked, although men and women usually have separate shower facilities. Topics such as menstrual problems (headaches, cramps) are frequently discussed quite openly. This openness about sex in the Netherlands has only existed since about 1970. Many Dutch see this as an important advance.

Homosexuality is also finding increasing acceptance in the Netherlands. Many homosexuals live openly as such.

You might be surprised, but, despite all this, there is still considerable shame and ignorance in the Netherlands with respect to sex.

22
Whistling at women on the street

If you're a foreign woman, you will have noticed that Dutch men do not openly show their appreciation for women in public. In France, Surinam, Turkey and Italy, a man lets a woman know he finds her attractive in several ways: prolonged stares, calling out or whistling.

Dutch men do not do this. Although they do look at women, they don't make it obvious. Dutch males consider it unseemly to whistle and call after women. A Dutch woman wouldn't appreciate it either. Her reply would be something like: 'You act like a construction worker or a road worker.'

23

Showing that you want sex

The Dutch usually show that they want sex in a fairly indirect way. A young man will almost never say to a girl: 'How about it, baby?' To a Dutch woman, that would be much too direct, too irreverent and *quite* unseemly.

A young man who wants to sleep with a girl employs a different tactic: talking to her at great length, but not about sex. Then he invites her to 'come to my place for a drink'. Or she asks him home for 'a cup of coffee'. This is a kind of code language. In most cases, the real motive is understood by both. But of course this 'beating around the bush' does lead to misunderstandings. A TV ad campaign and sex education at schools are attempting to combat misunderstandings by explaining that a girl might really mean *a cup of coffee*, and that she does not want sex at all.

24

Do Dutch women seem unfeminine to you?

Many foreign men and women find that Dutch women neither have a feminine appearance nor exhibit feminine behavior. In their eyes, Dutch women are far too masculine: they wear pants, have a manly gait and make little effort to be pleasing to men.

Many Dutch women find it silly and overdone to have their nails manicured, wear perfume, skirts or make-up, and, in general, to pay too much attention to clothes.

25

Breasts or buttocks?

In some non-Western countries, heterosexual men are especially attracted to women's buttocks, the fuller the better. Not so in the Netherlands. In general, the Dutch male is more a 'breast-man' than a 'buttock-man'. Dutch women with large buttocks are usually not happy about their appearance. They certainly will not wear brightly colored shorts to accentuate their buttocks.

26

Relationships: understanding, respect and love

In modern-day Holland, understanding, respect and love are considered vital components of a relationship. People want partners who really listen; they consider mutual understanding and respect for one another's feelings important.

Fifty years ago, when the Netherlands was a much poorer country, it was a different story. Back then, demands by one partner on the other were more *practical* than they are now. In those days, it was important to have a husband who did not drink too much or frequent prostitutes. He had to earn a decent income. The wife's virtues, on the other hand, were thrift (you didn't want a wife with 'a hole in her hand', *een gat in haar hand*) and the ability to raise children and mend clothing. Understanding, respect and love were less important back then.

27

How do the Dutch move their bodies?

Compared to many Surinamese and Antillians, Dutch people have stiff, angular body movements. The Dutch think their way of moving is normal; they find it 'overdone' to move the entire body rhythmically to music, even rhythmic music. Sometimes they feel jealous of others whose body movements are fluid and supple.

28
'Come in'

When you enter a Dutch home, not everybody will stand up. Sometimes people will stand up to shake your hand, but this is not obligatory. If people remain seated, do not interpret this as rudeness. Nor are *you* obliged to shake everyone's hand, unless this is your first visit. Your Dutch host will not give you an 'official welcome'.

You might find this manner of receiving guests uncivilized and rude, but to the Dutch this is simply a relaxed way of greeting visitors.

'Hi, everybody. I'm not going to go around shaking hands, it's too much trouble.'

29
Coffee

Coffee is an essential part of Dutch life. When the Dutch invite you to their homes, they often promptly serve you a cup of coffee or tea. Is this a hint that you should not stay too long? Quite the contrary: in Holland, a steaming *kopje koffie* is a hearty welcome. With each cup your host or hostess will offer you a cookie – one cookie, mind you – after which the lid goes back on the cookie tin. The Dutch see nothing uncongenial whatsoever in this ritual. Usually you will be offered a second cup of coffee, again with one cookie.

If you've had enough coffee, you can simply say so ('No, thanks. Maybe later.'). Do not lay your spoon on top of the cup, as you might be accustomed to. Your Dutch host may think this is impertinent.

When two Dutch people have something to discuss, a typical remark is: 'Shall we have some coffee?' This same expression is also used when the beverage is not coffee, but tea.

30

'Gezelligheid'

Not only coffee, but *gezelligheid* is an essential ingredient of Dutch society. When people reminisce about times gone by it is usually the *gezelligheid* they miss most of all. Dutch who live abroad and are homesick particularly miss the *gezelligheid* of Holland. It is difficult to pinpoint exactly what *gezelligheid* is. It has to do with feelings of snugness, coziness, security, serenity, homeyness and relaxation.
Drinking coffee can be *gezellig*. Visiting a friend can be *gezellig*. So can an open fire. A neighborhood can have a *gezellig* feel to it; a painting depicting a rustic setting can also be *gezellig*. If someone refers to you as *gezellig*, take this as a compliment.

31

At the table

Dutch table manners might be different from what you're used to. In the Netherlands, 'table etiquette' is as follows:
– After the meal you remain seated at the table to talk, 'napraten' or 'natafelen' in Dutch.
– After a meal at someone else's house, Dutch guests will say: 'Het heeft me goed gesmaakt' (I certainly enjoyed it) or 'Het was heerlijk' (It was delicious).
– It is considered very gracious to offer help in clearing the table. Your offer will probably be declined (also polite), but the fact that you offered is much appreciated. In the Netherlands it is not considered 'effeminate' for a man to help clear the table.

32

Television

When you visit Dutch people at home, they normally turn off the TV; this is a sign of good manners. They consider it quite unpleasant if the TV is left on while they are visiting someone: their host seems more interested in the television than in his guests!

A Dutchman:
'I visited some people the other day and it was dreadful. They left the television on the entire time. Can you imagine such a thing?'

33

Give my regards to your wife

In taking leave, a Dutch man will often remark: 'Give my regards to your wife.' This is to show that he has not forgotten his friend's wife in her absence. It has no sexual connotations. If a Dutchman makes this remark to you, an appropriate response would be: 'Thank you, I will.'

34

Helping a woman into her coat

If you (a man) and your wife visit Dutch friends, your Dutch host might get your wife's coat for her as you prepare to leave. He will hold the coat in such a way that your wife can slip into it with a minimum of effort.
You need not feel offended or uncomfortable when this happens. The Dutchman performing this ritual considers it a very polite gesture. Dutch men find helping a woman into her coat the height of courtesy.

35

Adapting to life in Holland

The Dutch sometimes say that foreigners should adapt to the way of life in Holland. It is their opinion that Dutch living abroad adapt to *their* host country.
But this is not always the case. Many Dutch in Benidorm, Spain, prefer to eat French fries and have a real Dutch dinner. The Dutch community in Australia has its own radio and television stations. And in the United States the many Dutch clubs are packed on 'Koninginnedag', the day on which the Queen's birthday is celebrated.
Do you know why some Dutch are opposed to European unification? They are afraid the Netherlands will have to conform too much to other E.U. countries!

36

Dogs and cats

Many Dutch people have a dog or a cat. Their owners buy expensive pet food for them and shower them with affection. Sometimes a dog is allowed to lick his master's face. Most people do not find that unhygienic; they love their dog. To the Dutch, a dog is not an unclean animal!
Pets are important to many people. They aren't as important as a child, but if a pet dies it is mourned by its owners. If a dog or cat dies, it is often buried or cremated. Dogs and cats are sometimes even allowed to get up on the table. Nor is this considered unhygienic.
Fifty years ago, affection for animals was not as strong in the Netherlands as it is today. In this respect, things have changed considerably since then.

The final sentence in a letter from a Dutch couple:
'Kisses to you from us both and a lick from Hector' (the dog).
This is not said to give offense; it expresses affection. It shows that not only people are important in Dutch society, but animals as well.

37
Religion

To many Dutch, religion is not very important. If you ask them if they believe in God, they say it does not really matter to them whether God exists.
What the Dutch *do* find important, though, is living an honest life, taking others into account, being fair, and so on. But to them these qualities are entirely separate from God or religion.
Most Dutch do not believe it is God's will when something serious happens. They see it as a chance occurrence that could just as easily *not* have happened.
Fifty years ago the Dutch were a far more religious people than they are today.

38
Which hand: left or right?

In Holland, people give you things with either hand, right or left. Most Dutch do not even notice the difference. They do not have a special hand for personal hygiene or prayer, or for touching unclean things or preparing food. In daily life, they use both hands for everything.

39
Pork or beef?

Most Dutch eat any kind of meat; they don't care if it's pork, chicken, or beef. They do not feel an aversion to pork as Moslems do. The aversion Hindus have to beef is even stranger to the Dutch.
There are Dutch who do not eat pork, but that's because they believe it is bad for the complexion. Christianity no longer prescribes what its followers should eat. Until about 1960, Dutch Catholics were not allowed to eat meat on Fridays, but this rule no longer applies.

40

Conversations

The Dutch feel that conversations should proceed calmly. Even when you disagree, it is important to maintain your composure. To the Dutch, the normal way to converse is to stay calm and not use your hands excessively. They find an emotional style of conversing rather trying. They want you to hold your hands still and discuss matters without raising your voice. Nor should you make extreme statements, even when something is very important to you.

To the Dutch, even a moderate display of emotion can be seen as excessive. They are afraid that an argument or fight will ensue.

41

Getting straight to the point

When the Dutch have to discuss a difficult topic, their usual approach is to plunge right into it. They hardly even take the time to sit and relax. They do not gradually work up to the difficult subject, but come straight to the point.

To you this probably makes a blunt and tactless impression. In some regions of the Netherlands (Limburg and the Eastern Netherlands) the people are more reticent and begin with small talk ('koetjes en kalfjes', 'cows and calves', a typical Dutch expression) before introducing the real topic.

(42)

Direct language: contradicting one another

If the Dutch do not agree with something, they make this known in a very direct way. A pupil can say to his teacher: 'Sir, you're wrong' or 'Sir, you've made a mistake'. This is not considered rude in the Netherlands. In fact, this type of direct confrontation is considered very positive. Perhaps you find it impertinent, but to the Dutch this type of response is both polite *and* direct.
They often make these critical remarks within earshot of others. Young people are permitted to contradict their elders, but they must proceed with care.

(43)

Telling the truth versus lying

Honesty may very well be the characteristic the Dutch value most in themselves. They want you to 'tell it like it is', even when it's painful, when that truth is blunt or impertinent, or when others will get hurt by it. Dutch people will not appreciate it if you tell a 'white lie' to avoid putting someone in an awkward position. They think that's dishonesty, lying. The great emphasis on honesty in Dutch culture is even reflected in a TV commercial in which milk is referred to as 'an honest dairy product'.

(44)

In what situations do the Dutch not tell the truth?

Though the Dutch think of themselves as always telling the truth, this is not the case. Dutch people 'lie' in the following situations:

- What do you think of my new dress? Isn't it pretty?
  It's a match made in heaven.
- Do I have bad breath?
  What do you mean? I don't smell a thing.

– Is everything all right with you?

Couldn't be better. And you?

– Or is it sex you're after?

Not at all. Where did you get that idea?

45

Arguments and opinions

When you ask the Dutch for their opinion, they start by giving you their opinion, then follow it up with supporting arguments. For example: 'I think it's a very good idea because...' *You* would probably start with the arguments, *then* give your opinion. This is very confusing to the Dutch. They ask your opinion and you begin with arguments. Often your conversation partner will already have stopped listening by that time because he thinks: She's beating around the bush, or: He does not even *have* an opinion.

Which is the Dutchman?
You ask: 'What do you think of viewpoint X?'
a. 'On the one hand I think... But on the other hand it's also true that... Which is why I think...'
b. 'I'm against it because I think...'

46

Why?

Dutch people very often ask: 'Why is that?' or 'Why do you do that?' That's quite normal in the Netherlands. It should not be interpreted as rudeness or impertinence; usually they are simply curious as to why you want a certain thing or why you do a certain thing.

In most cases, questions beginning with 'why' are not a sign of protest, but a request for information.

47

Asking for a promotion

Many Dutch literally ask for what they want. If, for example, an employee wants a promotion, it's quite common to ask for it point-blank. In many other cultures, this kind of request would not be appropriate. Instead, you would really throw yourself into your work which would make it obvious that you want a better position.
If a foreigner in the Netherlands works extra hard, his boss will think: 'He's working hard; he must be content.' Dutch bosses don't understand in such a situation that the foreign worker wants a promotion.

A Dutchman to his boss:
'I was wondering if I could move into a better position in the company.'

48

I don't know

You will have noticed that people in the Netherlands do not hesitate to say they do not know something. The Dutch do not consider this cause for embarrassment. In a similar situation, you might be used to pretending that you *do* know. The Dutch do not find it impolite or impertinent if you answer them with 'I don't know'.

49

They always want to stand out in the crowd

Do you think that Dutch people always want to stand out in the crowd? *They* don't look at it this way. Most Dutch would actually prefer *not* to draw attention to themselves. But they were taught at a very young age that it's important to have an opinion on a variety of topics. They were also taught that it's very important to openly express these opinions. To the Dutch that's quite normal. But to you, it seems that they are always trying to stand out in a crowd.

50

An argument has to be cleared up

After an argument, the Dutch will want to 'clear the air'. They'll want to discuss:
– Why did you do that?
– What did you think I meant at the time?
– What did *I* think that *you* meant?
– What were you feeling then? And so on.
Many Dutch will first want to thoroughly talk out the argument before they 'let bygones be bygones'. An argument that has not been cleared up is not officially over.

51

Not too enthusiastic

The Dutch are not very profuse in their reactions.
When they're satisfied, they prefer to say they are 'not dissatisfied'.
A much-enjoyed film will be called 'not bad'.
If they think highly of an idea, they'll say: 'Yes, there's something to that.'
How are things at work? 'I can't complain.'

52

Taking the initiative

The Dutch consider it very important that people take initiative themselves instead of waiting around until someone says: 'Could you do this?' The Dutch will really appreciate it if you investigate legislation, seek contacts, become familiar with customs, organizations, and so on. In their eyes, most foreigners are too passive. This often irritates them.

53

Making jokes about the royal family

The Dutch regularly make jokes about their royal family. But they are less inclined to accept the same thing from you as a foreigner.

It's rather like making negative remarks about one's own family. People do not accept hearing their own critical remarks echoed by outsiders.

54

Teasing

Many Dutch enjoy teasing each other. When you tease someone you deliberately take little jabs at his honor. For example, Dutch men are particularly sensitive to the insinuation that they are henpecked. And jokes meant to tease often concern the henpecked husband:

'How irritating! I don't seem to have any money with me. Could you lend me some?'
'Oh? Didn't your wife give you any pocket money this week?'

Usually when the Dutch tease each other they don't mean any harm. Teasing is a sign that a person likes you; it means that a friendship is growing between you. The 'teaser' isn't trying to pick a fight! The Dutch often make a game out of countering each teasing remark with an even better remark of their own. However, sometimes even the Dutch don't like to be teased. In the Netherlands, men are more apt to tease than women. Inhabitants of big cities tease more than rural people.

55

A gift for the boss

If you bring a gift for your boss when you return from vacation, he might react strangely. Your colleagues will probably also look up in surprise. They think you're asking for a favor.
In the Netherlands it is not customary to bring a gift for the boss. To you it's just a sign of respect, but that's not how it comes across.

56

Emancipated women

In Holland, women are allowed to do just about everything men do. Dutch men are proud of that. Women are allowed to go to cafés, choose any profession they want, contradict men in public, have an opinion of their own, and so on.
The Dutch often find it irritating when they see a Moroccan or Turkish woman walking two meters behind her husband. To them this is not only backward, but also degrading to the woman in question. To an extent, however, equality of the sexes in the Netherlands is an illusion. Emancipation for women didn't really make any headway until after 1970. And precisely because emancipation for women is so new in the Netherlands, the Dutch find it doubly irritating to see their not-so-old ways mirrored in foreigners.

57
Wives and daughters

The Dutch are also proud of their wives and daughters, but they express it differently. Girls are allowed to go out alone at night, even with boys they hardly know. The fear of a daughter losing her virginity before marriage is no longer an issue for Dutch parents.
Dutch men don't think their wives and daughters constantly need the protection of a man. If a brother and sister go to a party, their parents feel more concerned for their daughter than their son, but this has more to do with a fear of sexual assault. This explains why daughters are often fetched and brought home afterwards. The idea of a daughter sleeping with several men before she marries does not concern most Dutch parents anymore.

'I'd rather my daughter have several sexual partners before she marries. I had to find out all those things after I got married.'

58
A woman boss

In recent years the Dutch have begun to find it increasingly normal to have a woman as a boss. Yet a male boss still has an easier time: his subordinates are more apt to believe what he says and his orders are carried out more promptly. People in Holland who want to be progressive act as if it's perfectly normal to have a woman as a boss.

59

'Me' culture, 'we' culture

Dutch culture is often called a 'me' culture. What does that mean? A few examples:
– If you ask a Dutchman if he believes in God, he'll stop to think about it. This means that everyone will give a different answer.
– Dutch parents teach their children: 'It doesn't matter what others think of you. All that counts is what *you* think of yourself.'
– If the son in a Dutch family steals, this is not a disgrace to the father and brother. It is only a disgrace to the son, because he is the one who did it. In a 'we' culture, the entire family is disgraced if a son steals. In such a culture, people sometimes say that the parents are at fault if the son steals. To the Dutch this is quite unreasonable.
– Dutch people do not strike up conversations with strangers at the bus stop. Most people don't say a word in the train either.
– In the bus or train, most Dutch look for a seat as far away from others as possible. You hardly see any people sitting together!
– In general, the Dutch don't mind being alone for a while. In fact, they even enjoy it: this is the Dutch need of privacy. Dutch people who visit Morocco, for example, feel the need to be alone from time to time. Their Moroccan hosts, on the other hand, want to keep them company all day long. If the Dutchman says he wants to be alone, his Moroccan host will think he isn't enjoying the visit. But this isn't the case. The Dutch simply have a greater need of privacy.

60

'My child's upbringing is none of your business'

If you catch somebody else's child destroying something, you probably find it perfectly normal to tell that child off. Many Dutch would take offense at this. They feel you should stay out of it: it's *their* child.

(61)

Body contact

In Holland, strangers do their best to avoid touching each other. When they want to sit or walk past others, they will take care to maintain a small space between their bodies. Women in particular do this, but men do as well.
At a crowded party, people sometimes cannot avoid making body contact. If two people's legs accidentally touch, those involved will draw their legs back and say: 'Excuse me.' In the bus or train, people also do their best to avoid bodily contact. In very crowded situations where people cannot avoid pressing against each other, they will excuse themselves: 'Sorry about that. It certainly is full here, isn't it?'
Dutch people who are uncomfortable when someone sits very close to them will deliberately choose a chair (instead of the couch) when visiting a Moroccan family, for example. This should not be interpreted as arrogance.

(62)

Dutch friends do not always have time for you

Dutch friends do not always have time for you. Perhaps you will find this confusing. For example, a Dutch friend might say: 'I don't have time for you tonight.' That doesn't mean he's cross with you. Your friend simply wants to do something else tonight and will have time for you another day.
The Dutch would also rather not be disturbed at certain moments. Someone who's reading the newspaper, for example, will want to finish his article. Only then will he have time for you.

Do you understand why the Dutch sometimes feel that 'foreigners' make a request in a demanding, pushy manner?

63
Reluctance to get on each other's nerves

The Dutch do not want to 'get on each other's nerves'. This means refraining from talking too loudly in the waiting room or the train, for example. Neighbors do not want to hear each other, so you have to be careful not to turn the TV or radio on too loudly at home. For the same reason, doors must not be slammed, but closed gently.
You will probably think the Dutch get on each other's nerves for the slightest thing.

64
'Give me the salt!'

This is how Surinamese and Turks ask for the salt during a perfectly normal, *gezellig* meal. Hearing this, a Dutchman will think: 'Nobody's going to tell *me* what to do!' To him this is a rude way of asking. He probably won't say so, but he feels offended.
A Dutchman who wants the salt might say:
– 'Could I have the salt?' Or:
– 'Would you mind passing me the salt?' Or:
– 'Pass the salt, please.'

65
'Don't be silly'

A major argument once broke out at a company when a Dutch boss said to a foreign worker: 'Don't be silly' (the Dutch expression, *'doe niet zo gek'*, could literally be translated as 'don't act so crazy'). The worker thought his boss was calling him crazy and a major conflict arose.
This expression is always meant in a kindly way. The Dutch only use it when they like you.

There are quite a few other expressions that may lead to misunderstandings.
Do you know what it means – and how seriously it's meant – when someone says the following to you:
– *'What are you staring at?' (the Dutch expression,* 'heb ik wat van je aan', *literally means 'am I wearing something of yours?')*
– *'Cut the play-acting' (*'Stel je niet aan, joh!'*)*
– *'Don't be such a fool' (*'Doe niet zo idioot!'*)*
– *'Are you totally out of your mind?' (*'Ben je nou helemaal belazerd?'*)*
– *'Up yours' (*'Ach krijg het heen en weer'*)?*

66

Now you're really one of us

There are a number of words and expressions that the Dutch don't expect you to be familiar with. You'll notice the wonder in their eyes when you mention participating in 'the Annual Four-Day Walking Event', say that your child loves 'apekooien' (a gymnastic children's game), that you're going to the 'aubade' on the Queen's Birthday, or that you're learning songs for 'Sint-Maarten', Martinmas.

There are also certain turns of phrase that the Dutch will not expect from you. Ask how old someone's child is, for example. Whatever the age, remark: 'What a lovely age.' That has a very Dutch ring to it!

67

What do they talk about?

When two Dutch strangers get talking, they see nothing unusual in asking each other questions such as: What kind of work do you do? Where do you live? Do you like living there? These are not considered private matters.

Perhaps they will ask you similar questions. They assume that other people also find it normal to inquire about these matters.

68

How much do you earn?

In Holland – even with someone you know very well – it is not acceptable to ask how much a person earns. The Dutch do not ask this question either, although they *are* curious about your bank account and income.

69

Movements and gestures

A Dutchman who is calling you might make a movement with his hand which is deeply offensive to you: as if you are a dog being chased away.
You are not being treated like a dog. This is a case in which a gesture has a different meaning in two different cultures. A wink of the eye, for example, does not usually indicate sexual interest. It may mean: 'Do you get my joke?' A Dutchman complimenting you on your intelligence (by tapping his finger on the right side of his head) is making a gesture that you think means: 'You're out of your mind.' If a Dutchman wants to tell you you're out of your mind, he'll point to the *middle* of his forehead.

70

Looking into each other's eyes

The Dutch find it quite normal to maintain extended eye contact during a conversation. Men also do this when talking to women. To the Dutch this is not considered impolite. Nor does it convey sexual interest. Children are taught to look their parents or teacher in the eye when talking to them. If a shopkeeper avoids looking at a Dutch customer, the customer will think: The shopkeeper doesn't want my business.
If you avoid people's glances in Holland, they might think you're up to no good or that you have something to hide. A Dutch child who is honest (or wants to create that impression) will look you right in the eye and say (for example): 'I didn't do it. Honestly.' If something has been stolen, the child who refuses to meet your gaze will automatically be considered guilty.

71
Confessing to the crime

If a Dutchman is caught stealing, he will always admit to the theft. He might say, for example: 'You're right, I did take it.' That's expected of a person who stole something.
The Dutch get very angry with Moroccans and Turks who refuse to confess to a crime they have committed. Police and teachers in particular get furious when they catch Achmed red-handed and he refuses to admit to the theft.
When a Dutchman makes a mistake, he might say, for instance: 'Sorry, I was wrong.' A boss can also admit having been wrong to his employees. Most Dutch find that quite normal.

72
First a warning, then punishment

In the Netherlands, it is quite common not to punish someone the first time he breaks a law, but to let him off with a warning. Even the police often choose not to penalize a criminal for his first theft; they give him a 'warning' instead. This means: 'The first time you'll be forgiven, but if it happens again you'll be punished.' And they mean it! To most Dutch, a warning is a kind of punishment in itself.

73
Showing remorse: 'I won't do it again'

In Holland, when a person steals something, he is expected to feel remorse. A person who feels remorse wishes afterwards that he hadn't done what he did. Remorse also implies a resolution not to do it again in the future. That is why someone who feels remorse says: 'I'll never do it again.' If a person is truly sorry, his conscience makes him feel guilty for what he did.
True remorse, therefore, does not mean you tarnished the family honor because you were found out. It means your own conscience makes you feel guilty .
Many foreigners seem to have a feeling of shame in such situations, shame that the theft was found out. The Dutch, however, expect the culprit to feel guilty.

(74)

Apologizing

If a Dutchman has done something he regrets, he will apologize for his behavior. He might say, for instance: 'I shouldn't have done it', 'My apologies', 'Sorry' or 'Forgive me'.
In the Netherlands, a great deal of importance is placed on offering your apologies. You do this if you have hurt or inconvenienced a person in some way. If you do not openly offer your apologies, it appears as if you do not really regret your actions.

(75)

It's what you meant that counts

When people have had a major argument and are talking it out afterwards, the most important consideration is: what was your intention? A person can say: 'Yes, that's what I said, but I *meant* something different from what you thought.' In this type of discussion what counts most is what was *meant*. To the Dutch, the emphasis is on what a person actually means: that's what he wants to be judged by.

(76)

Are there no social values in the Netherlands?

To foreigners it may sometimes appear that there are no social values in the Netherlands. This is not true, but it may seem that way.

Foreign children sometimes think they can do whatever they please at school. After all, at school it is all right to contradict the teachers, use the informal form of address ('je' and 'jij') and even throw wads of paper through the classroom.

It is always difficult for foreigners to figure out what the values actually are in a new country. The Dutch cannot tell you what their values are either, because they are usually unwritten rules.

(77)

Smacking your lips at the table

Do you ever eat at the house of Dutch friends? As children they learned that it is offensive to smack their lips at the table. To a Dutchman, eating in a mannerly fashion means not making any noise and chewing with the mouth closed. You shouldn't be able to look into a Dutchman's mouth while he's eating.

Do you think they aren't enjoying the food? That's not the case. It's just that the eating habits they were taught are different from yours. The Dutch refer to their eating habits as 'table manners'. They find it terribly unpleasant if you smack your lips or slurp your tea. Drinking must also be done silently.

(78)

Ritualistic spitting

Most Dutch find spitting vulgar. If you are a Moslem, you will want to rinse your mouth before prayer, and it is forbidden to swallow this water. Dutch who are unfamiliar with Islamic ways sometimes find it irritating when Moslems spit in the sink. It might be a good idea to explain why you rinse your mouth.

(79)

Outings

In the Netherlands it is quite common for employees of a company to go on outings together, for example to a bowling alley or restaurant. Company employees also go out to dinner together when the company has something to celebrate, for example a tenth or twenty-fifth anniversary.

(80)

Are the Dutch unpredictable?

Do you find the Dutch unpredictable? This is probably because you are still unfamiliar with Dutch customs, norms and values. The Dutch, in turn, often find foreigners unpredictable. This is because they know very little about you.
Don't jump to the conclusion that the Dutch are unpredictable. Try to find out what their rules are.

You have a computer. Everything goes wrong with it. What is your reaction?
– 'This machine is unpredictable' or:
– 'Something has gone wrong; I'm not familiar with the way it works.'

81
Insurance

The Dutch seem to fear the future. Almost every Dutchman has several types of insurance: health insurance, home insurance, personal liability, fire and theft insurance, pension insurance, even 'funeral insurance'.
They have no choice. If their house burns to the ground, their family won't pay for a new house, even if they have the means to do so. If they lose their income due to injury or illness, help from family members and neighbors will be negligible.
'You should have had insurance', is the standard Dutch response.

82
The telephone

When answering the phone, the Dutch response will be something like: 'Jansen speaking'. If they are storeowners, they will answer with: 'Good morning, Jansen's Grocer's.' The Dutch always begin by telling you their names and expect you to do the same when they dial your number.
If you have an answering machine, the standard type of message in Holland is:
'This is the answering machine of Mr/Mrs X. Please leave a message after the beep. Clearly state your name and telephone number and I will ring you as soon as possible.'

83

Meetings

Perhaps you'll become a member of the employees council at your company or join the parents' committee at your children's school. In that case, it's handy to know the following. The Dutch have a very fixed approach to conducting meetings. Here are a number of rules usually adhered to during meetings:

- Each meeting is begun by agreeing which topics will be discussed. Those topics are referred to as 'items on the agenda'. The topics themselves and the order in which they will be presented are called 'the agenda'. While a particular item is being presented, the Dutch only discuss things relevant to that item. Only after that subject has been formally concluded will the other topics be dealt with.

  Perhaps in your native country you are accustomed to a less rigidly structured style of conversation.
- If you wish to discuss a particular topic, you must mention this to the chairman beforehand. You may raise a minor item for discussion at the beginning of the meeting. Quite often you will be asked to express your concerns or opinion in writing. In other words, it is not permitted to raise a new topic (item on the agenda) during the meeting. If you do so, a Dutch chairman (if he's doing his job) will say: 'That is not on our agenda for today. We have not had the opportunity to prepare for it.'
- The Dutch often begin by stating their own opinion. Only later on, when decisions must be made, do they take others' ideas into account.
- If people at the meeting disagree, it is considered important to reach a 'compromise'. A compromise means that everyone gives in a little; no one gets his way entirely, but everyone is satisfied and the meeting can continue.

84
Anti-German

Many Dutch are anti-German. When they see a German, they may say (half jokingly) to each other: 'I want my bike back.' This refers to the fact that, as World War II neared its end, some Germans attempted to flee back to Germany on bicycles stolen from the Dutch.
Anti-German remarks from you, a foreigner, will be slightly confusing to the Dutch.

85
Belgians

Every country has jokes about a particular group of people who are reputed to be particulary stupid. For the Turks they are the Laz people, in Germany the East Frisians. The Dutch assign this role to the Belgians. The Belgians, in turn, tell jokes about Dutch stinginess.

A Belgian joke:
Q: 'How do you know when a Belgian has been correcting a computer text?'
A: 'By the white correction fluid on the screen!'

86
Having versus sharing

Many foreigners say that the emphasis in the Netherlands is on *having*, that the Dutch are not inclined to share. Often, when a Dutchman in need of money goes to his well-off brother, the brother will say: 'Go borrow it from the bank.'
If a Dutchman has a full pack of cigarettes, it is not acceptable to simply reach over and take one. You have to ask permission first. Even if a Dutchman has plenty of cigarettes, he would

find it impertinent if you simply took one.
Dutch friends eating cookies in the train will not offer them to a stranger sitting nearby. Each person eats his own portion.

87

Keeping professional and private matters separate

In differences of opinion or disputes, the Dutch find it important to make a distinction between professional and private matters. If a Dutchman has a sharp disagreement with a colleague during a meeting, he will not think it strange to go and have a drink with that person afterwards.
Their rationale is that 'you have to make a distinction between professional matters (the cause of the argument) and private matters. In other words, you can disagree professionally yet continue to be friends on a personal level. That is how the Dutch like to see it, but they themselves do not always succeed in maintaining this division.

88

Expressing emotions

The Dutch do not find it easy to express their emotions. In the Netherlands it's never really accepted to fly into a rage; crying is only really 'permitted' shortly after a death or a divorce. They *talk* about their emotions more than they express them. In a conflict situation the Dutchman must also continue to behave 'correctly'. His conscience as well as his culture prevent him from becoming emotional. As a result, the Dutch remain angry for a long time after a conflict. They haven't expressed their rage, so they harbor a grudge. After a conflict, they will often 'talk the situation over', but in doing so they never give their feelings free rein.

89

The birthday calendar

Many Dutch have a 'birthday calendar' at home, usually hanging on the inside of the bathroom door. On this calendar the birthdays of family and friends are mentioned. If your name appears on this calendar they think quite highly of you!
On a son or daughter's birthday the entire family is 'congratulated' (wished 'happy birthday'), not only the birthday boy or girl. But only the person whose birthday it is gets gifts.

90

'Sinterklaas'

Sinterklaas (the feast of St. Nicholas) is an important Dutch holiday. It is celebrated each year on December 5th. *Sinterklaas* is not considered by the Dutch to be a Christian holiday.
Though *Sinterklaas* himself bears a striking resemblance to a bishop, to the Dutch he is simply a wise old man with a beard. All Dutch (except Jehovah's Witnesses) celebrate *Sinterklaas*, even if they're not religious.
On *Sinterklaas*, Dutch people give presents to each other, often accompanied by a short rhyme. These rhymes often contain playfully worded criticism, directed at the person receiving the present. *Zwarte Piet* (Black Peter) is a simple-minded, inarticulate black attendant of St. Nicholas' ('I not can talk good'). Many dark-skinned Dutch people object to this figure because they think he reinforces stereotypes about blacks. Usually the Dutch do not particularly want to hear this kind of criticism: it's *their* holiday.

91
Christmas

In recent years, an increasing number of Dutch people have begun giving gifts on Christmas (December 25th). This holiday has also lost its Christian significance for many people. They barely remember that Christmas is held to commemorate the birth of Jesus Christ. To them, the Christmas tree is not a symbol of Christianity, but of the cozy feeling surrounding Christmas.

92
Sending Christmas and New Years' cards

If you want to make a very Dutch impression, send Christmas and New Years' cards in December. Just about everyone sends these cards in Holland, to family and business contacts alike. The card will bear a message along the lines of: 'Merry Christmas and a Happy New Year'. It is important to keep track of those people who send you Christmas cards. You should send them a card as well.

93

Here's to your health!

In the Netherlands a person's health is very important. You can see this in the way they toast and in the way they tell each other off. When toasting, they say: 'To your health.' But when telling each other off, the Dutch wish each other all kinds of terrible diseases: 'get typhoid', 'get cholera', and so on. They also call each other *kankerlijer* (literally: someone riddled with cancer) or *etterbak* ('a person full of pus').
In your world, honor holds a more prominent place. You toast to 'honor'; when you tell someone off, you call his mother a whore, marking him a 'son of a bitch'.

94

The wish list

In the weeks before *Sinterklaas* and as their birthdays draw near, children make up a wish list. On the list, they write down what they would like to receive.
When people marry, they often have a wish (or 'gift' list). This list will either be present at a particular store or at the home of the bride's or groom's parents. People who want to give the bridal couple a gift refer to the list and choose an item in the price range they have in mind. Then that particular gift gets crossed off the list. Many Dutch find this procedure lacking in spontaneity, but the practice is growing in popularity. With a wish list, you never get the same gift from three different people.

95

Unwrapping presents

In the Netherlands, the rules for unwrapping gifts are changing. It used to be obligatory to unwrap everything at once, but when there are many gifts – at a wedding, for example – you simply can't open all of them. In that case, the name of the giver is written on the gift. The gift is unwrapped later and a thank-you card is sent to its giver.

On their birthdays, however, the Dutch are expected to unwrap their gifts. Whether or not they actually like the gift they exclaim: 'Oh, how lovely. Thank you very much.' If they already have that particular gift, it's fairly usual to say, for example: 'I already have this book. Did you keep the receipt? Then I can exchange it.'

96

Living together

In the last twenty years or so, it has become common practice for Dutch couples to live together before marriage. The Dutch feel it's better for people to get to know each other first. And a growing number of parents allow their son or daughter to have a girlfriend or boyfriend sleep over.
Around 1960 premarital sex for women would have been absolutely unthinkable in the Netherlands; it was the worst disgrace parents could be faced with. The daughter was thought to be no better than a whore. In those days, when a girl had a child out of wedlock, her family would insist that she marry right away. It was a disgrace to the entire family.
These days, more and more brides are already pregnant when they walk down the aisle. In this area, values are changing rapidly in Dutch society.

97

Family celebrations are contracted out

In the Netherlands, weddings and a number of other festivities include a meal for guests. These meals are not prepared by the family. Instead, the Dutch will pay a restaurant to prepare a meal and organize the celebration from start to finish. If a company throws a large party to celebrate its 25th anniversary, it is not organized by the company employees. Either a catering company will be engaged or they will all go out somewhere together.

98

Saving stamps

Many Dutch save stamps. These stamps are provided with the purchase of ten liters of gasoline or 25 guilders' worth of groceries. They are taken home and saved up in booklets. If you hand in 250 stamps, for example, you can get a cup and saucer for half price. If you hand in HFL 12.50 in coupons, some stores will give you a coupon for a 15-guilder train ticket. The Dutch greatly appreciate it if you save stamps or coupons for them. In particular demand are the 'points' found on coffee wrappers.

99

Last but not least: frugality

The Dutch are well aware of their frugal reputation in other countries. It's best not to rub it in. They themselves often do not know what to think of the frugal Dutch mentality. But they won't mind if you laugh at their 'waste not' devices: the cheese slicer, the tiny spatula to scrape out the last of the yogurt or *vla* in a bottle, or the potato peeler.

On the one hand, the Dutch are proud of their thrift: they disapprove of people who throw money around. But on the other hand they are ashamed of being called 'frugal'.

A Dutch joke:
'Why do Dutch men groan when they come?'
'Because it has to come from their own zak*' (sack, scrotum, which also means 'pocket' in Dutch).*

This joke isn't only amusing to you (the frugality rings a bell), but to the Dutch as well. They laugh at it because it's about sex and they enjoy the play on words.

Finally: Does anyone have a 100th tip?
Is dealing with the Dutch even more difficult than I have suggested?
Send your tips to:

ACTA Midden Nederland
Postbus 14007
3508 SB, Utrecht
The Netherlands

I would appreciate it!

Hans Kaldenbach
ACTA Midden Nederland

ACTA Midden Nederland is an organization and consultancy specialized in managerial and counseling issues.

ACTA specializes in:
* *Intercultural advice*
* *Intercultural management training*
* *Training concerning the multicultural work-place*
* *Intercultural educational training*
* *'Train the trainer' workshops*
* *Courses on career advancement for foreign employees.*